Editor
Gisela Lee, M.A.

Managing Editor
Karen Goldfluss, M.S. Ed.

Editor-in-Chief
Sharon Coan, M.S. Ed.

Illustrator
Howard Chaney

Cover Artist
Barb Lorseyedi

Art Director
CJae Froshay

Art Coordinator
Kevin Barnes

Imaging
Rosa C. See

Product Manager
Phil Garcia

Publisher
Mary D. Smith, M.S. Ed.

GRADE 3

Author
Mary Rosenberg

Teacher Created Resources, Inc.
6421 Industry Way
Westminster, CA 92683
www.teachercreated.com

ISBN: 978-0-7439-3743-6

©2003 Teacher Created Resources, Inc.
Reprinted, 2008
Made in U.S.A.

Table of Contents

The old adage "practice makes perfect" can really hold true for your child and his or her education. The more practice and exposure your child has with concepts being taught in school, the more success he or she is likely to find. For many parents, knowing how to help your children can be frustrating because the resources may not be readily available. As a parent it is also difficult to know where to focus your efforts so that the extra practice your child receives at home supports what he or she is learning in school.

This book has been designed to help parents and teachers reinforce basic skills with children. *Practice Makes Perfect* reviews basic math skills for children in grade 3. While it would be impossible to include all concepts taught in grade 3 in this book, the following basic objectives are reinforced through practice exercises. These objectives support math standards established on a district, state, or national level. (Refer to the Table of Contents for specific objectives of each practice page.)

- adding and subtracting
- multiplying and dividing
- adding and subtracting money
- numbers
- measurement

- using fractions
- using standard form
- finding the area and volume
- finding important information
- decimals and place value

There are 36 practice pages. (*Note*: Have children show all work where computation is necessary to solve a problem. For multiple choice responses on practice pages, children can fill in the letter choice or circle the answer.) Following the practice pages are six test practices. These provide children with multiple-choice test items to help prepare them for standardized tests administered in schools. As your child completes each test, he or she can fill in the correct bubbles on the optional answer sheet provided on page 46. To correct the test pages and the practice pages in this book, use the answer key provided on pages 47 and 48.

How to Make the Most of This Book

Here are some useful ideas for optimizing the practice pages in this book:

- Set aside a specific place in your home to work on the practice pages. Keep it neat and tidy with materials on hand.
- Set up a certain time of day to work on the practice pages. This will establish consistency. Look for times in your day or week that are less hectic and more conducive to practicing skills.
- Keep all practice sessions with your child positive and constructive. If the mood becomes tense, or you and/or your child are frustrated, set the book aside and look for another time to practice.
- Help with instructions if necessary. If your child is having difficulty understanding what to do or how to get started, work through the first problem with him or her.
- Review the work your child has done. This serves as reinforcement and provides further practice.
- Allow your child to use whatever writing instruments he or she prefers. For example, colored pencils can add variety and pleasure to drill work.
- Pay attention to the areas in which your child has the most difficulty. Provide extra guidance and exercises in those areas. Allowing children to use drawings and manipulatives, such as coins, tiles, game markers, or flash cards, can help them grasp difficult concepts more easily.
- Look for ways to make real-life applications to the skills being reinforced.

Practice 1

Read each event and decide whether it is likely to happen or unlikely to happen. Circle the word.

1. Raising my allowance

Likely   Unlikely

2. Taking a test today

Likely   Unlikely

3. Cleaning my desk

Likely   Unlikely

4. Watching cartoons at school

Likely   Unlikely

5. Staying up late tonight

Likely   Unlikely

6. Cleaning my bedroom

Likely   Unlikely

7. Eating hot lunch

Likely   Unlikely

8. Walking the family pet

Likely   Unlikely

9. Eating brownies for dinner

Likely   Unlikely

10. Doing my homework

Likely   Unlikely

Practice 2

Write each number in standard form.

1. Abyssinians

2,000 + 300 + 80 + 3

_____

2. American Shorthairs

1,000 + 30 + 2

_____

3. Birmans

900 + 30 + 3

_____

4. Exotic Shorthairs

1,000 + 900 + 80 + 1

_____

5. Maine Coons

4,000 + 700 + 40 + 7

_____

6. Ocicats

800 + 60 + 8

_____

7. Oriental Shorthairs

1,000 + 300 + 70 + 1

_____

8. Persians

40,000 + 2,000 + 500 + 70 + 8

_____

9. five hundred twenty-eight

10. three thousand, six hundred, fifty

11. one hundred twenty-six

12. six thousand, four hundred, eighty-one

_____ _____ _____ _____

Practice 3

Write each number in standard form.

1. Beagles fifty-six thousand, nine hundred, forty-six _____ 	**2.** Cocker Spaniels forty-five thousand, three hundred five _____ 
3. Dachsunds forty-eight thousand, four hundred twenty-six _____ 	**4.** German Shepherds seventy-nine thousand, seventy-six _____ 
5. Golden Retrievers sixty-eight thousand, nine hundred ninety-three _____ 	**6.** Pomeranians thirty-nine thousand, seven hundred twelve _____ 
7. Poodles fifty-six thousand, eight hundred three _____ 	**8.** Rottweilers eighty-nine thousand, eight hundred, sixty-seven _____ 

Identify the place value of the underlined digit.

9.   **10.**   **11.**   **12.**

61,10<u>3</u>   <u>5</u>6,257   2<u>9</u>,446   98,<u>4</u>74

_____   _____   _____   _____

Practice 4

Rewrite the height of each mountain in standard form.

1. Gannett Peak   10,000 + 3,000 + 800 + 4 feet   _____ feet

2. Mt. Elbert   10,000 + 4,000 + 400 + 30 + 3 feet   _____ feet

3. Mt. McKinley   20,000 + 300 + 20 feet   _____ feet

4. Mt. Rainier   10,000 + 4,000 + 400 + 10 feet   _____ feet

5. Mt. Whitney   10,000 + 4,000 + 400 + 90 + 4 feet   _____ feet

Using the information from above, circle the highest mountain.

6. Mt. Whitney   **7.** Mt. McKinley   **8.** Gannet Peak

   Mt. Elbert   Mt. Rainier   Mt. Whitney

   Mt. McKinley   Mt. Elbert   Mt. Rainier

Use the numbers 1, 2, and 3 to rank the mountains in order from shortest to highest.

9. _____ Gannett Peak   **10.** _____ Mt. Whitney   **11.** _____ Mt. Rainier

   _____ Mt. Elbert   _____ Mt. Rainier   _____ Mt. McKinley

   _____ Mt. McKinley   _____ Gannett Peak   _____ Mt. Elbert

Practice 5

Use the numbers 1–10 to rank the rivers in order from **longest** to **shortest**.

_____	Arkansas	1,396 miles	_____	Red	1,018 miles
_____	Columbia	1,210 miles	_____	Rio Grande	1,885 miles
_____	Mississippi	2,348 miles	_____	St. Lawrence	760 miles
_____	Missouri	2,315 miles	_____	Snake	1,083 miles
_____	Ohio	981 miles	_____	Yukon	1,979 miles

1. Which river is longer than the Missouri River?_____

2. Which river is shorter than the Ohio River? _____

3. Which river is longer than the Columbia River and shorter than the Rio Grande?

   _____

4. Which river is longer than the Red River and shorter than the Columbia River?

   _____

5. How many rivers are longer than 1,500 miles? _____

6. How many rivers are longer than 1,000 miles but less than 1,500 miles? _____

7. How many rivers are shorter than 1,000 miles? _____

Use the length of each river to write and solve each math problem.

8. Arkansas + Yukon + Snake = _____   9. Mississippi + Red + Ohio = _____

10. Missouri – Yukon = _____   11. Columbia – St. Lawrence = _____

Practice 6

Shade in the correct amount on each circle to show the equivalent fractions.

1.  $\frac{1}{2} = \frac{3}{6}$	**2.** $\frac{1}{1} = \frac{5}{5}$	**3.** $\frac{2}{3} = \frac{6}{9}$
4. $\frac{2}{4} = \frac{4}{8}$	**5.** $\frac{1}{3} = \frac{2}{6}$	**6.** $\frac{2}{3} = \frac{4}{6}$

Use the > (greater than), < (less than), or = (equal to) symbols to compare each set of fractions.

7. $\frac{2}{5} \bigcirc \frac{8}{9}$	**8.** $\frac{1}{3} \bigcirc \frac{1}{6}$	**9.** $\frac{1}{4} \bigcirc \frac{2}{8}$
10. $\frac{3}{6} \bigcirc \frac{1}{2}$	**11.** $\frac{1}{1} \bigcirc \frac{6}{7}$	**12.** $\frac{2}{4} \bigcirc \frac{3}{4}$

Practice 7

1. Write the fraction for the shaded part.

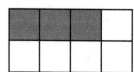

_____

2. Write the fraction for the shaded part.

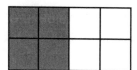

_____

3. Write the fraction for the shaded part.

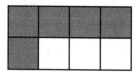

_____

4. Write the fraction. Write < or > to compare the fractions.

_____ ◯ _____

5. Write the fraction. Write < or > to compare the fractions.

_____ ◯ _____

6. Write the mixed fraction.

_____

7. Write the mixed fraction.

_____

8. Write the mixed fraction.

_____

9. Rewrite each fraction as a mixed fraction.

$\frac{9}{7}$ = _____ $\frac{14}{3}$ = _____

10. Rewrite each fraction as a mixed fraction.

$\frac{7}{2}$ = _____ $\frac{6}{5}$ = _____

Practice 8

Complete the chart.

Coin	Number Needed to Make $1.00	Fraction of $1.00
1. half dollar	2	1/2 of a $1.00
2. quarters		
3. dimes		
4. nickels		
5. pennies		

Write each amount using a dollar sign and a decimal point.

6. Four dollars eighty-three cents _____

7. Thirty-nine dollars seventy-six cents _____

8. Two hundred eighty-one dollars ten cents _____

Rewrite each amount in standard monetary form.

9. 310/100 _____   **10.** 1274/100 _____

11. 5911/100 _____   **12.** 462/100 _____

Read each word problem. Write the money in two ways—as a fraction of a dollar and with a dollar sign and decimal point.

13. Gloria has 5 dimes, 1 nickel, and 6 pennies.

_____/100   or $ ___. ___ ___

14. Sean has 2 quarters, 2 nickels, and 5 pennies.

_____/100   or $ ___. ___ ___

15. Linda has 8 dimes and 7 nickels.

_____/100   or $ ___. ___ ___

16. Bart has 1 half dollar, 1 quarter, and 10 pennies.

_____/100   or $ ___. ___ ___

Practice 9

Rewrite each improper fraction as a mixed fraction.

1.

$\frac{3}{2}$ or _____
gingerbread men

2.

$\frac{10}{3}$ or _____
wreaths

3.

$\frac{17}{4}$ or _____
candies

Rewrite each mixed fraction as an improper fraction.

4.

$5\frac{1}{2}$ or _____
fishing hats

5.

$2\frac{1}{6}$ or _____
flower petals

6.

$2\frac{1}{3}$ or _____
pennies

Circle the correct answer to each question.

1/4 cup

1/3 cup

1/2 cup

7. The recipe calls for 1 1/3 cups of flour.

A. $\frac{1}{2}+\frac{1}{2}+\frac{1}{3}$

B. $\frac{1}{4}+\frac{1}{4}+\frac{1}{2}$

C. $\frac{1}{3}+\frac{1}{3}+\frac{1}{3}$

8. Jay needs 3/4 of a cup of water.

A. $\frac{1}{4}+\frac{1}{3}$

B. $\frac{1}{3}+\frac{1}{3}$

C. $\frac{1}{4}+\frac{1}{2}$

9. Suzy used 2 cups of sugar.

A. $\frac{1}{4}+\frac{1}{4}+\frac{1}{2}+\frac{1}{2}$

B. $\frac{1}{2}+\frac{1}{2}+\frac{1}{2}+\frac{1}{2}$

C. $\frac{1}{3}+\frac{1}{3}+\frac{1}{4}+\frac{1}{2}$

10. Mom found 1 1/2 cups of walnuts.

A. $\frac{1}{3}+\frac{1}{3}+\frac{1}{3}$

B. $\frac{1}{2}+\frac{1}{2}+\frac{1}{2}$

C. $\frac{1}{4}+\frac{1}{4}+\frac{1}{4}+\frac{1}{4}$

Practice 10 ◐ ◑ ◐ ◑ ◐ ◑ ◐ ◑ ◐ ◑ ◐ ◐ ◑ ◐ ◑

1. What is the place value of the 8 in 857.01?

(A) tenths   (B) hundreds

(C) tens   (D) hundredths

2. What is the place value of the 9 in 432.96?

(A) hundredths   (B) tenths

(C) hundreds   (D) tens

3. What is the place value of the 4 in 942.85?

(A) tens   (B) ones

(C) hundreds   (D) tenths

4. What is the place value of the 3 in 107.63?

(A) tens   (B) hundreds

(C) hundredths   (D) tenths

5. What is the place value of the 9 in 617.94?

(A) hundreds   (B) tens

(C) tenths   (D) hundredths

6. What is the place value of the 2 in 352.61?

(A) tens   (B) ones

(C) tenths   (D) hundreds

7. What is the place value of the 8 in 497.08?

(A) tenths   (B) hundreds

(C) hundredths   (D) tens

8. What is the place value of the 2 in 162.89?

(A) ones   (B) tens

(C) tenths   (D) hundreds

9. What is the place value of the 9 in 537.96?

(A) tens   (B) hundreds

(C) tenths   (D) hundredths

10. What is the place value of the 1 in 957.81?

(A) hundreds   (B) tens

(C) tenths   (D) hundredths

Practice 11

---

1. Write the fraction for one section.

_____

2. Write the fraction for one section.

_____

3. Write the fraction for one section.

_____

---

4. Circle $\frac{1}{2}$ of the pictures. Write the answer.

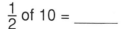

$\frac{1}{2}$ of 10 = _____

5. Circle $\frac{1}{3}$ of the pictures. Write the answer.

$\frac{1}{3}$ of 9 = _____

---

6. Write the fraction for one section.

_____

7. Write the fraction for one section.

_____

8. Write the fraction for one section.

_____

---

9. Divide the pictures into 3 equal sets. Complete the problem.

$\frac{2}{3}$ of 12 = _____

10. Divide the pictures into 6 equal sets. Complete the problem.

$\frac{3}{6}$ of 12 = _____

Practice 12

Write and solve each addition problem.

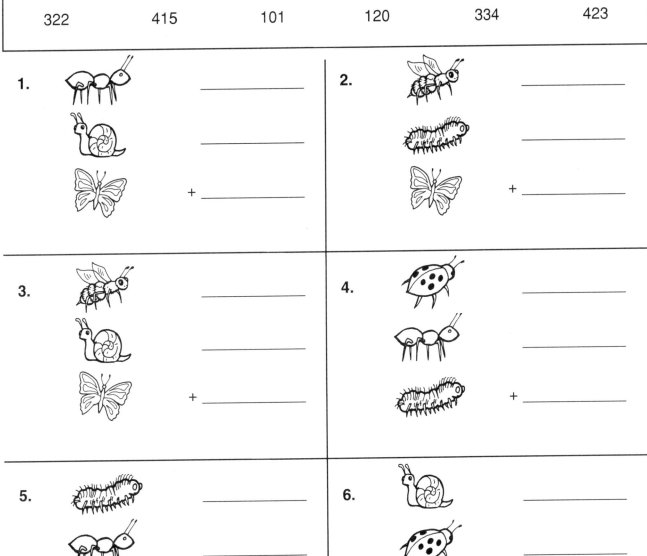

© *Teacher Created Resources, Inc.*   *#3743 Practice Makes Perfect: Math Review*

Practice 13

Use the > (greater than) or < (less than) symbol. Write the place (ones, tens, hundreds, thousands, ten thousands) for the digits that were compared.

Example

<u>5</u>,198 (<) <u>8</u>,458

_____thousands_____

1.

5,67<u>7</u> ◯ 5,67<u>9</u>

_____

2.

7,<u>1</u>36 ◯ 7,<u>3</u>13

_____

3.

42,4<u>5</u>4 ◯ 42,4<u>1</u>4

_____

4.

32,5<u>0</u>2 ◯ 32,5<u>1</u>2

_____

5.

74,898 ◯ 73,101

_____

6.

10,57<u>6</u> ◯ 10,57<u>9</u>

_____

7.

<u>4</u>1,911 ◯ <u>3</u>5,611

_____

8.

72,125 ◯ 78,687

_____

Read and solve the word problem.

9. Devin has 6,461 bottle caps. Jimmy has 3,219 more bottle caps than Devin. Stella has 1,038 fewer bottle caps than Jimmy. How many bottle caps do Jimmy and Stella have?

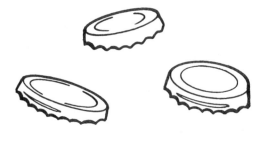

Jimmy has _____ bottle caps. Stella has _____ bottle caps.

Practice 14 ᵔ ❂ ᵔ ❂ ᵔ ❂ ᵔ ❂ ᵔ ❂ ᵔ ᵔ ❂ ᵔ ❂

Use the given set of digits to make the different kinds of numbers.

Example: 3, 4, 9, 1	**1.** 5, 2	**2.** 7, 4
largest: _____9,431_____ smallest: _____1,349_____ odd: _____1,943_____ even: _____9,134_____	largest: _____ smallest: _____ odd: _____ even: _____	largest: _____ smallest: _____ odd: _____ even: _____
3. 1, 0, 2	**4.** 9, 6, 1	**5.** 1, 1, 2
largest: _____ smallest: _____ odd: _____ even: _____	largest: _____ smallest: _____ odd: _____ even: _____	largest: _____ smallest: _____ odd: _____ even: _____
6. 8, 6, 3, 4	**7.** 1, 2, 9, 3	**8.** 6, 3, 5, 3
largest: _____ smallest: _____ odd: _____ even: _____	largest: _____ smallest: _____ odd: _____ even: _____	largest: _____ smallest: _____ odd: _____ even: _____

Use the numbers you created in problems 1–8 to answer each question.

9. What was the largest number made? _____

10. What was the smallest number made? _____

11. Write a number that was less than 500. _____

12. Write a number that was more than 500 and less than 1,000. _____

13. Write a number that was more than 1,000 and less than 5,000. _____

14. Write a number that was more than 5,000. _____

Practice 15 ꙮ

Round each planet's number of revolutions around the sun for each problem.

1. Round to the nearest hundred.

Mercury 88 days

_____

2. Round to the nearest hundred.

Venus 224.7 days

_____

3. Round to the nearest hundred.

Earth 365.36 days

_____

4. Round to the nearest thousand.

Jupiter 4,332.6 days

_____

5. Round to the nearest ten thousand.

Saturn 10,759.2 days

_____

6. Round to the nearest ten thousand.

Pluto 90,950 days

_____

Use the rounded numbers about planet revolutions from the problems above to solve each problem below.

7. Add.

Mercury + Pluto = _____

8. Subtract.

Pluto − Saturn = _____

9. Add.

Earth + Jupiter = _____

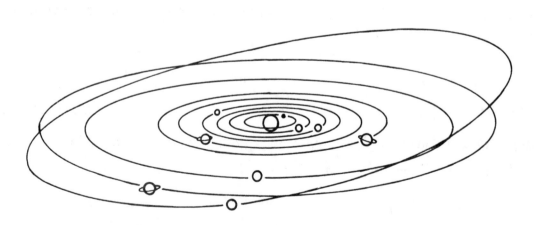

Practice 16 ꧁ ꧂ ꧁ ꧂ ꧁ ꧂ ꧁ ꧂ ꧁ ꧂ ꧁ ꧁ ꧁ ꧂ ꧁ ꧂

Identify the missing piece of information in each word problem.

1. Henry bought 3 boxes of cupcake mix. Each mix will make 6 cupcakes. Will there be enough cupcakes for the party?

   Missing information: _____

2. Louisa has been saving her money for 3 months. Now she has $15.00! Does she have enough to buy the roller blades?

   Missing information: _____

3. There are 25 families who have signed up for movie night. The cafeteria can hold 150 people. Will there be enough room for everyone?

   Missing information: _____

4. Sammy caught some fly balls. Tammy caught 10 more fly balls than Sammy. How many fly balls did Tammy catch?

   Missing information: _____

5. Vincent has 15 pets. He has 6 cats, some dogs, and some hamsters. How many hamsters does Vincent have?

   Missing information: _____

6. Kelsey brought $10 to the snack bar. She bought a hot dog, some chips, a soda, and a candy bar. How much change was Kelsey given?

   Missing information: _____

Practice 17

| 90°
Right Angle
A right angle makes a corner.
A right angle is 90°. |  < 90°
Acute Angle
An acute angle is < 90° (is less than 90°). |  > 90°
Obtuse Angle
An obtuse angle is > 90° (is greater than 90°). |

Circle the answer that best describes the angle.

1.

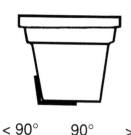

< 90°   90°   > 90°

2.

< 90°   90°   > 90°

3.

< 90°   90°   > 90°

Follow the directions.

4. Circle the *right* triangle.

5. Draw a line under the *obtuse* triangle.

6. Make an x on the *acute* triangle.

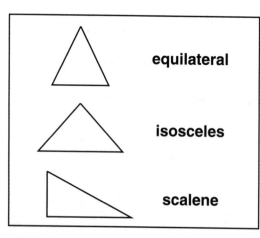

equilateral

isosceles

scalene

Which Triangle Am I?

7. Only two of my sides are congruent (equal in length). Which triangle am I?

_____

8. None of my sides are congruent (equal in length). Which shape am I? _____

9. All of my sides are congruent (equal in length). Which shape am I? _____

Practice 18

Line	Line Segment
• A line is straight.	• A line segment is straight.
• A line goes on forever in both directions.	• A line segment has 2 endpoints.
	• A line segment is part of a line.

• The line is read as: line ST or line TS.	• The line segment is read as line segment AB or line segment BA.
• The line is written as $\overleftrightarrow{ST}$ or $\overleftrightarrow{TS}$.	• The line segment is written as $\overline{AB}$ or $\overline{BA}$.

Circle the correct answer.

1.

line   line segment

2.

line   line segment

3.

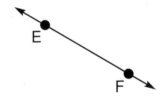

line   line segment

Identify each line or line segment by circling the correct answer.

4.

$\overline{GH}$ $\overleftrightarrow{GH}$

5.

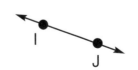

$\overline{IJ}$ $\overleftrightarrow{IJ}$

6.

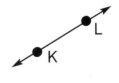

$\overline{KL}$ $\overleftrightarrow{KL}$

Practice 19

The perimeter of a geometric figure is the distance around the figure. The perimeter can be computed by adding the lengths of all sides of the figure. The perimeter of most shapes is computed by adding the lengths of each side. In this example, the square has 4 equal sides. Each side is 6 feet long so the perimeter would be 4 x 6 feet = 24 feet.

6 ft.

Calculate the perimeter for each shape.

1.
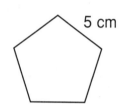
5 cm

P = _____

2.
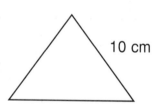
10 cm

P = _____

3.

4 ft.

P = _____

4.

8 in.

P = _____

5.
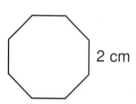
2 cm

P = _____

6.
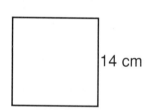
14 cm

P = _____

7.

7 ft.

P = _____

8.
9 in.

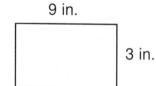
3 in.

P = _____

Practice 20

Find the area for each shape. Use the formulas to help you.

Square	**Rectangle**
Area = (length x width)	Area = (length x width)

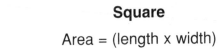

width
2 units

Area = (2 x 2)
Area = 4 sq. units

length = 2 units

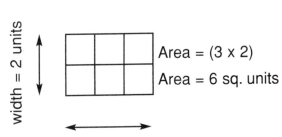

width = 2 units

Area = (3 x 2)
Area = 6 sq. units

length = 3 units

1.

4 units

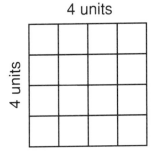

4 units

length = _____ units

width = _____ units

Area = _____ x _____

Area = _____ square units

2.

6 units

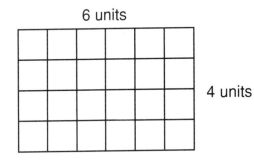

4 units

length = _____ units

width = _____ units

Area = _____ x _____

Area = _____ square units

3.

5 units

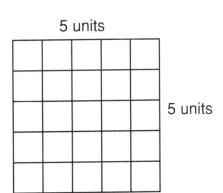

5 units

length = _____ units

width = _____ units

Area = _____ x _____

Area = _____ square units

4.

2 units

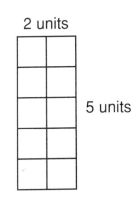

5 units

length = _____ units

width = _____ units

Area = _____ x _____

Area = _____ square units

Practice 21

Find the area for each triangle. Use the formula to help you.

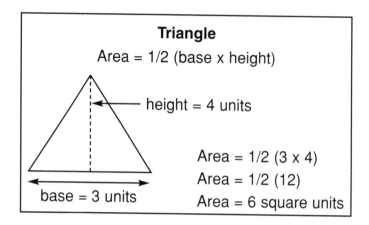

Triangle

Area = 1/2 (base x height)

height = 4 units

Area = 1/2 (3 x 4)
Area = 1/2 (12)
Area = 6 square units

base = 3 units

1.

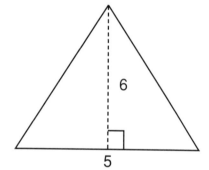

6

5

Base = _____ units
Height = _____ units
Area = 1/2 (_____ x _____)
Area = _____ square units

2.

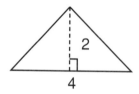

2

4

Base = _____ units
Height = _____ units
Area = 1/2 (_____ x _____)
Area = _____ square units

3.

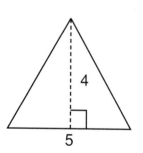

4

5

Base = _____ units
Height = _____ units
Area = 1/2 (_____ x _____)
Area = _____ square units

4.

2

2

Base = _____ units
Height = _____ units
Area = 1/2 (_____ x _____)
Area = _____ square units

Practice 22 ৶ Ꙭ ৶ Ꙭ ৶ Ꙭ ৶ Ꙭ ৶ ৶ Ꙭ ৶ Ꙭ ৶ Ꙭ

Use the formulas to find the volume for each one of the shapes.

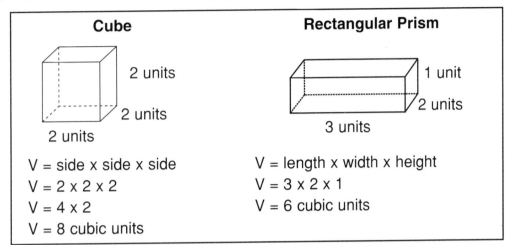

Cube

2 units
2 units
2 units

V = side x side x side
V = 2 x 2 x 2
V = 4 x 2
V = 8 cubic units

Rectangular Prism

1 unit
2 units
3 units

V = length x width x height
V = 3 x 2 x 1
V = 6 cubic units

1.

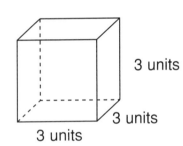

3 units
3 units
3 units

V = _____ x _____ x _____
V = _____ x _____
V = _____ cubic units

2.

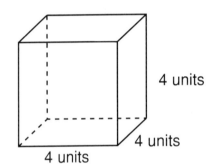

4 units
4 units
4 units

V = _____ x _____ x _____
V = _____ x _____
V = _____ cubic units

3.

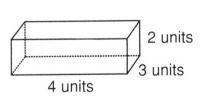

2 units
3 units
4 units

V = _____ x _____ x _____
V = _____ cubic units

4.

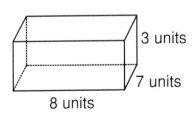

3 units
7 units
8 units

V = _____ x _____ x _____
V = _____ cubic units

Practice 23

Compete the chart.

X	0	1	2	3	4	5	6	7	8	9	10
0	0					0					0
1		1				5				9	
2			4			10			16		
3				9		15		21			
4					16	20	24				
5	0	5	10	15	20	25	30	35	40	45	50
6					24	30	36				
7				21		35		49			
8			16			40			64		
9		9				45				81	
10	0					50					100

Use the > (greater than), < (less than), or = (same as) symbols.

1. 5 x 1 ◯ 10 x 2

2. 3 x 1 ◯ 8 x 3

3. 4 x 7 ◯ 9 x 5

4. 6 x 2 ◯ 2 x 6

5. 6 x 9 ◯ 7 x 9

6. 8 x 7 ◯ 4 x 1

Practice 24 ❧ ❧ ❧ ❧ ❧ ❧ ❧ ❧ ❧ ❧ ❧ ❧ ❧ ❧

Solve each multiplication problem. Use each answer's letter to discover a secret question and its answer.

1. 14 x 2 ___ = W	**2.** 331 x 2 ___ = I	**3.** 4,244 x 2 ___ = T	**4.** 321 x 3 ___ = N	**5.** 212 x 4 ___ = L
6. 3,412 x 2 ___ = M	**7.** 313 x 3 ___ = A	**8.** 441 x 2 ___ = H	**9.** 3,142 x 2 ___ = P	**10.** 2,211 x 4 ___ = ?
11. 324 x 2 ___ = U	**12.** 2,332 x 3 ___ = C	**13.** 1,322 x 3 ___ = !	**14.** 1,241 x 2 ___ = Y	**15.** 4,123 x 2 ___ = O

___ ___ ___   ___ ___ ___
28 882 8,246   6,996 939 963

___ ___ ___ ___ ___ ___ ___ ___ ___
6,824 648 848 8,488 662 6,284 848 2,482 8,844

___   ___ ___ ___ ___
662   6,996 939 963 3,966

Practice 25

1,162	2,131	1,415	3,143	1,224	1,431

Write and solve each math problem.

1.  x 2 = ☐   **2.** x 3 = ☐   **3.** x 3 = ☐

4. x 4 = ☐   **5.** x 4 = ☐   **6.** x 4 = ☐

Do the operation in parentheses first.

7.

(x 4) − = ☐

8.

(+) x 1 = ☐

9.

(x 2) + = ☐

10.

+ (x 2) = ☐

Practice 26 ৩ ৩ ৩ ৩ ৩ ৩ ৩ ৩ ৩ ৩ ৩ ৩ ৩ ৩ ৩

Complete each table.

Example: ÷ 2	
4	2
2	1
6	3
8	4

1.

÷ 3	
9	
6	
15	
12	

2.

÷ 6	
12	
6	
24	
18	

3.

÷ 8	
8	
48	
24	
40	

4.

÷ 4	
16	
8	
40	
32	

5.

÷ 7	
49	
35	
70	
14	

6.

÷ 9	
36	
90	
45	
81	

7.

÷ 5	
15	
25	
35	
50	

Write the correct divisor for each table.

8.

÷ _____	
27	9
18	6
6	2

9.

÷ _____	
7	7
4	4
1	1

10.

÷ _____	
6	1
60	10
36	6

11.

÷ _____	
70	10
35	5
14	2

Practice 27

Find the unit cost for each item at each store. Circle the better deal.

Item	We Cost U Less	Bigger is Better	Best Unit Price
1.	1 crayon for $.80	5 crayons for $3.00	_____ each
2.	1 disk for $.10	7 disks for $2.10	_____ each
3.	1 pencil for $.10	6 pencils for $1.20	_____ each
4.	1 slice for $2.00	7 slices for $5.60	_____ each
5.	1 bag for $3.50	2 bags for $5.00	_____ each
6.	1 box for $.35	5 boxes for $1.25	_____ each
7.	1 deck for $.70	2 decks for $.90	_____ each
8.	1 book for $6.80	4 books for $60.00	_____ each

Practice 28

Solve these division problems.

1.

25 mittens in 6 groups   Remainder: yes   no

2.

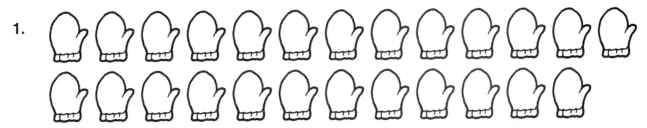

21 shoes in 7 groups   Remainder: yes   no

3.

20 hats in 3 groups   Remainder: yes   no

4.

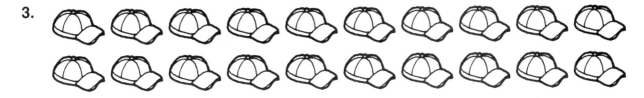

18 tickets in 3 groups   Remainder: yes   no

5.

28 candies in 10 groups   Remainder: yes   no

Practice 29 ⟀ ❧ ⟀ ❧ ⟀ ❧ ⟀ ❧ ⟀ ❧ ⟀ ❧ ⟀ ❧ ⟀ ❧ ⟀

Read and solve each word problem.

1. Janie made 9 necklaces. Each necklace had 3 beads on it. How many beads were used?

_____ beads were used.

2. Ralph made 2 boxes. In each box he put 10 baseball cards. How many cards were there in all?

_____ cards in all.

3. Sarah made 9 dog bones for each one of her 2 dogs. How many dog bones were there in all?

_____ dog bones in all.

4. Sherman sold 5 tickets. Each ticket cost $4.00. How much money did Sherman collect?

Sherman collected _____.

5. Perry corrected 10 papers. On each paper Perry made 4 stars. How many stars in all?

_____ stars in all.

6. Melinda had 9 bags. In each bag she put 6 rocks. How many rocks in all?

_____ rocks in all.

7. Rutger made 8 cinnamon rolls for each one of his 4 favorite customers. How many cinnamon rolls in all?

_____ cinnamon rolls in all.

8. Lisa bought 6 books of stamps. Each book contained 8 stamps. How many stamps in all?

_____ stamps in all.

Practice 30 ꙮ ꙮ ꙮ ꙮ ꙮ ꙮ ꙮ ꙮ ꙮ ꙮ ꙮ ꙮ ꙮ ꙮ ꙮ

Read and solve each word problem.

1. Abe used 96 toothpicks to build 3 model homes. How many toothpicks were used to build each home?

_____ toothpicks were used.

2. Ralph made 6 bags of pebbles. He had 72 pebbles in all. How many pebbles were in each bag?

_____ pebbles in each bag.

3. Tina painted 32 flowers on 4 walls. How many flowers were on each wall?

_____ flowers were on each wall.

4. Wes counted 45 cars while walking 5 miles. How many cars did he see for each mile?

Wes saw _____ cars for each mile.

5. There were 10 players on 2 teams. How many players were on each team?

_____ players were on each team.

6. Danielle counted 40 ladybugs on 10 flowers. How many ladybugs were on each flower?

_____ ladybugs were on each flower.

7. There were 56 spots on 8 Dalmatians. How many spots were on each Dalmatian?

_____ spots on each Dalmatian.

8. There were 15 people sitting in the first 3 rows. How many people were in each row?

_____ people were in each row.

Practice 31 ꙮ ꙮ ꙮ ꙮ ꙮ ꙮ ꙮ ꙮ ꙮ ꙮ ꙮ ꙮ ꙮ

Choose the correct answer.

1. Find the mystery number. The mystery number is an even number divisible by 3, 6, 11, and 33. What is the mystery number?

The mystery number is _____.

2. Lacy had $63.88. She spent $10.19 buying a new tire for her bike. How much money does Lacy have left?

Lacy has _____ left.

3. Lance wants to buy a new bike seat for $4.56 and a new tire pump for $19.54. What is the total cost for both items?

The total cost is _____.

4. The truck drove 500 miles on 10 gallons of gas. How many miles can the truck drive on one gallon of gas?

The truck can drive _____ on one gallon of gas.

5. In the last 3 basketball games, Antonia scored 15, 36, and 27 points. What was Antonia's average score?

Antonia's average score was _____.

6. Ginny had 10 ribbons. She sold each ribbon for 9¢. How much money did Ginny earn?

Ginny earned _____.

Practice 32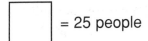

Use the chart to answer the questions.   = 25 people

1. How many people dream of going to a Dude Ranch?_____

2. Would more people like to sail around the world or travel by train? _____

3. How many people would like to travel by 5th wheel?_____

4. How many people want to go hiking? _____

Use the information from the chart to solve each problem.

5. hiking + dude ranch = _____

6. train x 3 = _____

7. 5th wheel ÷ 5 = _____

8. sailing x 4 = _____

9. trains – dude ranch = _____

10. 5th wheel – sailing = _____

Division

Practice 33

Use the pictures to help you solve each division problem and to find the remainder.
(R = remainder)

1.

    $10 \div 6 =$ ___ R ___

2.

    $9 \div 2 =$ ___ R ___

3.

    $10 \div 4 =$ ___ R ___

4.

    $8 \div 3 =$ ___ R ___

5.

    $7 \div 3 =$ ___ R ___

6.

    $9 \div 4 =$ ___ R ___

7.

    $8 \div 5 =$ ___ R ___

8.

    $7 \div 2 =$ ___ R ___

9.

    $10 \div 7 =$ ___ R ___

10.

    $10 \div 3 =$ ___ R ___

#3743 Practice Makes Perfect: Math Review

Practice 34 ꙮ ꙮ ꙮ ꙮ ꙮ ꙮ ꙮ ꙮ ꙮ ꙮ ꙮ ꙮ ꙮ ꙮ

Solve each division problem. Use each answer's letter to discover the secret message.

1. $5\overline{)16}$ D	**2.** $4\overline{)19}$ O	**3.** $3\overline{)11}$ V
4. $5\overline{)14}$ N	**5.** $3\overline{)20}$ I	**6.** $8\overline{)17}$ S
7. $5\overline{)21}$ P	**8.** $5\overline{)18}$!	**9.** $7\overline{)17}$ A

_____ _____ _____ _____ _____ _____ _____ _____
3 R1   6 R2   3 R2   6 R2   2 R1   6 R2   4 R3   2 R4

_____ _____   _____   _____ _____ _____ _____ _____
6 R2   2 R1   2 R3   2 R1   2 R4   2 R3   4 R1   3 R3

Practice 35

Solve each problem. Color the boxes of the division problems that have a remainder. Do you see a pattern?

1. $3\overline{)965}$	**2.** $6\overline{)8,436}$	**3.** $9\overline{)7,410}$
4. $5\overline{)5,810}$	**5.** $5\overline{)178}$	**6.** $9\overline{)1,125}$
7. $6\overline{)5,912}$	**8.** $7\overline{)623}$	**9.** $5\overline{)7,443}$
10. $7\overline{)9,576}$	**11.** $4\overline{)918}$	**12.** $2\overline{)644}$

What kind of pattern did you make? _____

Practice 36

Choose the operation needed to solve each problem.

1. One box of cereal has 18 servings. How many servings in 22 boxes?

    +   −   X   ÷

2. Jason had $25.00. He spent $12.93 buying a new CD. How much money does he have left?

    +   −   X   ÷

3. There is a total of 50 coins in 10 rolls. How many coins are in each roll?

    +   −   X   ÷

4. Amy caught 18 fish. James caught 6 fewer fish than Amy. How many fish did James catch?

    +   −   X   ÷

5. There is a total of 60 hens in 10 hen houses. How many hens in each house?

    +   −   X   ÷

6. Each van can carry 9 people. How many people can 4 vans carry?

    +   −   X   ÷

7. Josh counted 30 cars. Sybil counted 7 more cars than Josh. How many cars did Sybil count?

    +   −   X   ÷

8. There is a total of 50 stars on 6 flags. How many stars in all?

    +   −   X   ÷

9. There is a total of 32 paper clips in 4 boxes. How many paper clips in each box?

    +   −   X   ÷

10. Yesterday it was 97° F. Today it is only 80° F. What is the difference in temperature?

    +   −   X   ÷

Test Practice 1

1. Every Saturday afternoon Nadine goes to see the latest movie playing at the Good Times Movie Theater. Today is Saturday. What is the chance that Nadine will go to see a movie this afternoon?

    Likely   Unlikely
     (A)   (B)

2. Write the number in standard form.

8 ten thousands + 9 thousands + 8 hundreds + 7 tens + 6 ones

   9,876   89,876   89,706
   (A)   (B)   (C)

---

3. How much of the circle is shaded?

  1/4   1/2   3/4
  (A)   (B)   (C)

4. How much of the circle is shaded?

  1/3   1/2   1/6
  (A)   (B)   (C)

5. What is the time?

  1:55   2:55   11:10
  (A)   (B)   (C)

---

6. What is the place value of the underlined number?

3,9<u>8</u>7

   ten   thousand   hundred
   (A)   (B)   (C)

7. What is the place value of the underlined number?

<u>4</u>,256

   ten   thousand   hundred
   (A)   (B)   (C)

---

8. Identify the smallest fraction.

   1/4   1/3   1/6
   (A)   (B)   (C)

9. Identify the largest fraction.

   1/4   1/3   1/6
   (A)   (B)   (C)

Test Practice 2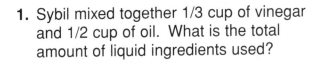

1. Sybil mixed together 1/3 cup of vinegar and 1/2 cup of oil. What is the total amount of liquid ingredients used?

$\frac{2}{3}$ cup
(A)

$\frac{4}{6}$ cup
(B)

$\frac{5}{6}$ cup
(C)

2. Bill had 4/5 of a cup of guacamole. He used 1/3 of a cup to make a guacamole sandwich. How much guacamole is left?

$\frac{7}{15}$ cup
(A)

$\frac{3}{10}$ cup
(B)

$\frac{3}{5}$ cup
(C)

3. Roma had 3/4 of a dollar. She spent $.18 buying a bike reflector. How much money does Roma have left?

72¢
(A)

57¢
(B)

61¢
(C)

4. John had half a dollar. He spent 23¢ buying a bike permit. How much money does John have left?

7¢
(A)

17¢
(B)

27¢
(C)

5. Muffins cost $3 for a dozen. Janell bought 1/2 a dozen. How much did she spend?

$1.25
(A)

$1.50
(B)

$1.75
(C)

6. What is the elapsed time?

20 min.
(A)

22 min.
(B)

25 min.
(C)

7. Rewrite this as an improper fraction. Becky ate 1 1/2 sandwiches.

$\frac{1}{2}$
(A)

$\frac{2}{3}$
(B)

$\frac{3}{2}$
(C)

8. Rewrite this as a mixed fraction. George bought 7/5 of a cake.

$1\frac{2}{7}$
(A)

$1\frac{2}{5}$
(B)

$1\frac{1}{7}$
(C)

Test Practice 3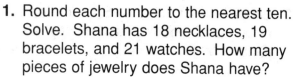

1. Round each number to the nearest ten. Solve. Shana has 18 necklaces, 19 bracelets, and 21 watches. How many pieces of jewelry does Shana have?

60	50	70
Ⓐ	Ⓑ	Ⓒ

2. Round each number to the nearest hundred.

Solve. At the Bike Fair, 307 handlebar streamers and 598 bike locks were given away. What was the total number of items given away?

1,000	600	900
Ⓐ	Ⓑ	Ⓒ

3. Identify.

line	line segment
Ⓐ	Ⓑ

4. Identify.

line	line segment
Ⓐ	Ⓑ

5. What is the largest number that can be made using 7, 1, 9, 0?

7,190	9,017	9,710
Ⓐ	Ⓑ	Ⓒ

6. A baby takes a 17-minute nap each day. If the baby lays down at 3:21, what time will the baby wake up?

3:38	3:48	3:28
Ⓐ	Ⓑ	Ⓒ

7. Add.

5,125 + 2,999 + 7,536

15,660	16,650	10,655
Ⓐ	Ⓑ	Ⓒ

8. Subtract.

74,576 − 64,488

10,088	12,008	11,008
Ⓐ	Ⓑ	Ⓒ

Test Practice 4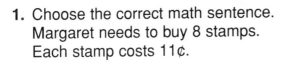

1. Choose the correct math sentence. Margaret needs to buy 8 stamps. Each stamp costs 11¢.

   8 x 11¢   8 x 1¢   8 x 8¢

   (A)   (B)   (C)

2. Ginny had 10 ribbons. She sold each ribbon for 9¢. How much money did Ginny earn?

   9¢   19¢   90¢

   (A)   (B)   (C)

3. Which is a longer period of time— 2 hours or 150 minutes?

   2 hours   150 minutes

   (A)   (B)

4. Find the area of the rectangle. (Area = length x width)

   3 units

   6 units

   18 sq. units   9 sq. units   36 sq. units

   (A)   (B)   (C)

5. Find the area of the triangle. (Area = 1/2 (base x height))

   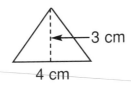
   3 cm
   4 cm

   24 cm   6 cm   15 cm

   (A)   (B)   (C)

6. Find the volume of the cube. (Volume = side x side x side)

   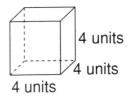
   4 units
   4 units
   4 units

   15   12   64
   cubic units   cubic units   cubic units

   (A)   (B)   (C)

#3743 Practice Makes Perfect: Math Review

Test Practice 5

1. A 6-pack of soda costs $2.04. What is the cost of one soda?

    25¢   31¢   34¢

    (A)   (B)   (C)

2. A 12-pack of gum costs $4.80. What is the cost of one pack of gum?

    40¢   4¢   50¢

    (A)   (B)   (C)

3. From the list below, find the mystery number.

61 62 63 64 65 66 67 68 69 70

The mystery number is an even number divisible by 3, 6, 11, and 33. What is the mystery number?

    61   63   66

    (A)   (B)   (C)

4. Solve.

8 cups of coffee can be made using 1 spoonful of coffee. If you need to make 80 cups of coffee, how many spoonfuls of coffee will you need to use?

    10   9   8

    (A)   (B)   (C)

5. Choose the correct math sentence. Gary bought 6 boxes of brownie mix. Each box makes 12 brownies. His twin sister, Cary made twice as many brownies as Gary. How many brownies did Cary make?

(A)   (6 x 2) x 12

(B)   (2 x 12) x 6

(C)   (6 x 12) x 2

6. Which number will have a remainder when divided by 3?

    9   19   39

    (A)   (B)   (C)

7. Which number will have a remainder when divided by 8?

    40   48   50

    (A)   (B)   (C)

Test Practice 6

1. Solve.

There are 36 pieces of licorice in a 6-ounce pack. How many pieces of licorice make up in one ounce?

3	6	9
(A)	(B)	(C)

2. Solve.

Brian rode his bike 8 miles and then ran for 2 miles. About how many kilometers (km) did Brian cover? (1 mile = 1.609 kilometers.)

10	16	19
(A)	(B)	(C)

3. Solve.

Ramona bought a notebook for $2.00, 3 pencils for $.30 each, and 2 erasers for $.15 each. How much money did Ramona spend?

$3.20	$4.12	$4.32
(A)	(B)	(C)

4. Solve.

Martin bought 4 pairs of socks for $11.39, and a pair of pants for $25. How much money did Martin spend?

$31.98	$22.89	$36.39
(A)	(B)	(C)

5. Solve.

Hilda bought 17 pencils to share with 4 friends. How many pencils can Hilda give to each friend? How many pencils will be left?

4 R1	5 R2	3 R3
(A)	(B)	(C)

6. Solve.

Jackson bought 51 dog bones to feed to 9 dogs. How many dog bones can each dog have? How many dog bones will be left?

4 R5	5 R6	3 R7
(A)	(B)	(C)

Answer Sheet

Test Practice 1

1. Ⓐ Ⓑ
2. Ⓐ Ⓑ Ⓒ
3. Ⓐ Ⓑ Ⓒ
4. Ⓐ Ⓑ Ⓒ
5. Ⓐ Ⓑ Ⓒ
6. Ⓐ Ⓑ Ⓒ
7. Ⓐ Ⓑ Ⓒ
8. Ⓐ Ⓑ Ⓒ
9. Ⓐ Ⓑ Ⓒ

Test Practice 2

1. Ⓐ Ⓑ Ⓒ
2. Ⓐ Ⓑ Ⓒ
3. Ⓐ Ⓑ Ⓒ
4. Ⓐ Ⓑ Ⓒ
5. Ⓐ Ⓑ Ⓒ
6. Ⓐ Ⓑ Ⓒ
7. Ⓐ Ⓑ Ⓒ
8. Ⓐ Ⓑ Ⓒ

Test Practice 3

1. Ⓐ Ⓑ Ⓒ
2. Ⓐ Ⓑ Ⓒ
3. Ⓐ Ⓑ
4. Ⓐ Ⓑ
5. Ⓐ Ⓑ Ⓒ
6. Ⓐ Ⓑ Ⓒ
7. Ⓐ Ⓑ Ⓒ
8. Ⓐ Ⓑ Ⓒ

Test Practice 4

1. Ⓐ Ⓑ Ⓒ
2. Ⓐ Ⓑ Ⓒ
3. Ⓐ Ⓑ
4. Ⓐ Ⓑ Ⓒ
5. Ⓐ Ⓑ Ⓒ
6. Ⓐ Ⓑ Ⓒ

Test Practice 5

1. Ⓐ Ⓑ Ⓒ
2. Ⓐ Ⓑ Ⓒ
3. Ⓐ Ⓑ Ⓒ
4. Ⓐ Ⓑ Ⓒ
5. Ⓐ Ⓑ Ⓒ
6. Ⓐ Ⓑ Ⓒ
7. Ⓐ Ⓑ Ⓒ

Test Practice 6

1. Ⓐ Ⓑ Ⓒ
2. Ⓐ Ⓑ Ⓒ
3. Ⓐ Ⓑ Ⓒ
4. Ⓐ Ⓑ Ⓒ
5. Ⓐ Ⓑ Ⓒ
6. Ⓐ Ⓑ Ⓒ

Answer Key

Page 4
Answers may vary.

Page 5
1. 2,383
2. 1,032
3. 933
4. 1,981
5. 4,747
6. 868
7. 1,371
8. 42,578
9. 528
10. 3,650
11. 126
12. 6,481

Page 6
1. 56,946
2. 45,305
3. 48,426
4. 79,076
5. 68,993
6. 39,712
7. 56,803
8. 89,867
9. ones
10. ten thousands
11. thousands
12. hundreds

Page 7
1. 13,804
2. 14,433
3. 20,320
4. 14,410
5. 14,494
6. Mt. McKinley
7. Mt. McKinley
8. Mt. Whitney
9. 1, 2, 3
10. 3, 2, 1
11. 1, 3, 2

Page 8
5 – Arkansas
6 – Columbia
1 – Mississippi
2 – Missouri
9 – Ohio
8 – Red
4 – Rio Grande

10 – St. Lawrence
7 – Snake
3 – Yukon
1. Mississippi
2. St. Lawrence
3. Arkansas
4. Snake
5. 4
6. 4
7. 2
8. 1,396 + 1,979 + 1,083 = 4,458 miles
9. 2,348 + 1,018 + 981 = 4,347 miles
10. 2,315 – 1,979 = 336 miles
11. 1,210 – 760 = 450 miles

Page 9
1.– 6. Check to make sure the student shaded the appropriate number of sections.
7. <
8. >
9. =
10. =
11. >
12. <

Page 10
1. 3/8
2. 4/8 = 1/2
3. 4/8 = 1/2
4. 2/5 < 3/5
5. 2/4 = 1/2 > 1/4
6. 3 2/4 = 3 1/2
7. 2 1/4
8. 1 1/5
9. 2 2/7, 4 2/3
10. 3 1/2, 1 1/5

Page 11
1. 2, 1/2 of $1.00
2. 4, 1/4 of $1.00
3. 10, 1/10 of $1.00
4. 20, 1/20 of $1.00
5. 100, 1/100 of $1.00
6. $4.83
7. $39.76

8. $281.10
9. $3.10
10. 1,274
11. 5,911
12. 462
13. 61/100 or $0.61
14. 65/100 or $0.65
15. 115/100 or $1.15
16. 85/100 or $0.85

Page 12
1. 1 1/2
2. 3 1/3
3. 4 1/4
4. 11/2
5. 13/6
6. 7/3
7. A
8. C
9. B
10. B

Page 13
1. B
2. B
3. A
4. C
5. C
6. B
7. C
8. A
9. C
10. D

Page 14
1. 1/2
2. 1/7
3. 1/9
4. 5
5. 3
6. 1/6
7. 1/3
8. 1/1
9. 8
10. 6

Page 15
1. 322 + 423 + 120 = 865
2. 415 + 334 + 120 = 869
3. 415 + 423 + 120 = 958
4. 101 + 322 + 334 = 757
5. 334 + 322 + 101 = 757
6. 423 + 101 + 415 = 939

Page 16
1. < ones
2. < hundreds
3. > tens
4. < tens
5. > thousands
6. < ones
7. > ten thousands
8. < thousands

9. Jimmy has 9,680 bottle caps (6,461 + 3,219 = 9,680). Stella has 8,642 bottle caps (9,680 – 1,038 = 8,642).

Page 17
1. 52; 25; 25; 52
2. 74; 47; 47; 74
3. 210; 102; 201; 102, 120, or 210
4. 961; 169; 691 or 619; 916 or 196
5. 211; 112; 211 or 121; 112
6. 8,643; 3,468; for the odd and even numbers a variety of answers is possible
7. 9,321; 1,239; for odd and even numbers a variety of answers is possible.
8. 6,533; 3,356; for odd and even numbers a variety of answers is possible.
9. 9,321
10. 25
11.–14. Answers will vary.

Page 18
1. 100
2. 200
3. 400
4. 4,000
5. 10,000
6. 90,000
7. 100 + 90,000 = 90,100
8. 90,000 – 10,000 = 80,000
9. 400 + 4,000 = 4,400

Page 19
Possible sample sentences are shown.
1. How many people are coming?
2. How much do the roller blades cost?

3. How many people are in each family?
4. How many fly balls did Sammy catch?
5. How many dogs does he have?
6. How much did the snacks cost?

Page 20
1. 90°
2. > 90°
3. < 90°
4. first triangle
5. last triangle
6. middle triangle
7. isosceles
8. scalene
9. equilateral

Page 21
1. line segment
2. line
3. line
4. $\overline{GH}$-line segment
5. $\overleftrightarrow{IJ}$-line
6. $\overleftrightarrow{KL}$-line

Page 22
1. 25 cm
2. 30 m
3. 24 ft.
4. 32 in.
5. 16 cm
6. 56 m
7. 70 ft.
8. 24 in.

Page 23
1. 16 square units
2. 24 square units
3. 25 square units
4. 10 square units

Page 24
1. 15 square units
2. 4 square units
3. 10 square units
4. 2 square units

Page 25
1. 27 cubic units
2. 64 cubic units
3. 24 cubic units
4. 168 cubic units

Answer Key (cont.)

Page 26

Reading the chart horizontally across.

Row 0: all answers are zero

Row 1: 0, 1, 2, 3, 4, 5, 6, 7, 8, 10

Row 2: 0, 2, 4, 6, 8, 10, 12 14, 16, 18, 20

Row 3: 0, 3, 6, 9, 12, 15, 18, 21, 24, 27, 30

Row 4: 0, 4, 8, 12, 16, 20, 24, 28, 32, 36, 40

Row 5: 0, 5, 10, 15, 20, 25, 30, 35, 40, 45, 50

Row 6: 0, 6, 12, 18, 24, 30, 36, 42, 48, 54, 60

Row 7: 0, 7, 14, 21, 28, 35, 42, 49, 56, 63, 70

Row 8: 0, 8, 16, 24, 32, 40, 48, 56, 64, 72, 80

Row 9: 0, 9, 18, 27, 36, 45, 54, 63, 72, 81, 90

Row 10: 0, 10, 20, 30, 40, 50, 60, 70, 80, 90, 100

1. <   3. <   5. <
2. <   4. =   6. >

Page 27
1. 28   9. 6,284
2. 662   10. 8,844
3. 8,488   11. 648
4. 963   12. 6,996
5. 848   13. 3,966
6. 6,824   14. 2,482
7. 939   15. 8,246
8. 882

Mystery question and answer: Who can multiply? I can!

Page 28
1. 2,830   7. 5,381
2. 9,429   8. 2,655
3. 4,293   9. 3,739
4. 4,648   10. 8,610
5. 4,896
6. 8,524

Page 29
1. 3, 2, 5, 4
2. 2, 1, 4, 3
3. 1, 6, 3, 5
4. 4, 2, 10, 8
5. 7, 5, 10, 2
6. 4, 10, 5, 9
7. 3, 5, 7, 10
8. 3
9. 1
10. 6
11. 7

Page 30
1. $.60
2. $.30
3. $.20
4. $.80
5. $2.50
6. $.25
7. $.45
8. $15.00

Better deals for the following item numbers:
We Cost U Less: 2, 3, 8
Bigger is Better: 1, 4, 5, 6, 7

Page 31
1. yes   4. no
2. no   5. yes
3. yes

Page 32
1. 9 x 3 = 27; 27 beads were used.
2. 2 x 10 = 20; 20 cards in all.
3. 9 x 2 = 18; 18 dog bones in all.
4. 5 x $4.00 = $20.00; Sherman received $20.00 in all.
5. 10 x 4 = 40; 40 stars in all.
6. 9 x 6 = 54; 54 rocks in all.
7. 8 x 4 = 32; 32 cinnamon rolls in all.
8. 6 x 8 = 48; 48 stamps in all.

Page 33
1. 96 ÷ 3 = 32; 32 toothpicks were used.
2. 72 ÷ 6 = 12; 12 pebbles were in each bag.
3. 32 ÷ 4 = 8; 8 flowers were on each wall.
4. 45 ÷ 5 = 9; Wes saw 9 cars for each mile.
5. 10 ÷ 2 = 5; 5 players were on each team.
6. 40 ÷ 10 = 4; 4 ladybugs were on each flower.
7. 56 ÷ 8 = 7; 7 spots were on each Dalmatian.
8. 15 ÷ 3 = 5; 5 people were in each row.

Page 34
1. 66
2. $53.69
3. $24.10
4. 50
5. 26
6. 90¢

Page 35
1. 25
2. sail around the world
3. 150
4. 200
5. 200 + 25 = 225
6. 75 x 3 = 225
7. 150 ÷ 5 = 30
8. 100 x 4 = 400
9. 75 − 25 = 50
10. 150 − 100 = 50

Page 36
1. 1 R4
2. 4 R1
3. 2 R2
4. 2 R2
5. 2 R1
6. 2 R1
7. 1 R3
8. 3 R1
9. 1 R3
10. 3 R1

Page 37
1. 3 R1
2. 4 R3
3. 3 R2
4. 2 R4
5. 6 R2
6. 2 R1
7. 4 R1
8. 3 R3
9. 2 R3

Secret message: Division is a snap!

Page 38
1. 321 R2
2. 1,406
3. 823 R3
4. 1,162
5. 35 R3
6. 125
7. 985 R2
8. 89
9. 1,488 R3
10. 1,368
11. 229 R2
12. 322

The pattern is a checkerboard.

Page 39
1. x
2. −
3. ÷
4. −
5. ÷
6. x
7. +
8. x
9. ÷
10. −

Page 40
1. A
2. B
3. B
4. B
5. B
6. A
7. B

8. C
9. B

Page 41
1. C
2. A
3. B
4. C
5. B
6. C
7. C
8. B

Page 42
1. A
2. C
3. A
4. B
5. C
6. A
7. A
8. A

Page 43
1. A
2. C
3. B
4. A
5. B
6. C

Page 44
1. C
2. A
3. C
4. A
5. C
6. B
7. C

Page 45
1. B
2. B
3. A
4. C
5. A
6. B